Walking to Bethlehem:
A Devotional Journey through Advent

Kathryn,

May the story of Christmas bring hope, peace, joy & love as you enter the Christmas season.

love
Carolyn

See page 154 for start dates

For all of the beautiful hearts who welcomed us into that first Advent celebration and journeyed with us, through many more.

And
For David, who works tirelessly on these projects and who helps me see the beautiful, holy and good, in life-giving traditions.

Thank-You.

Walking to Bethlehem:
A Devotional Journey through Advent

Katharine Barrett

Walking To Bethlehem:
A Devotional Journey Through Advent

by Katharine Barrett

Published by Fresh Ink Media
ISBN: 978-0-9880768-2-2

Cover Design by Katharine Barrett
Cover and interior photographs copyright 2012 by
Katharine Barrett

"The hinge of history is on the door of a Bethlehem stable."

- R. W. Sockman

Walking to Bethlehem

Table of Contents

Week One:

~ ~ ~ ~

A few years ago, I had to begin wearing prescription glasses. They made things so much clearer and easier to read! I noticed details I'd been missing, and images were sharper. Celebrating Advent is a bit like wearing new glasses. It gives us the chance to wander through a familiar, beautiful story and maybe notice things we hadn't seen before. It's a clear focus, a fresh perspective; the anticipation of Emmanuel's light illuminating our steps, our hearts.

Will you walk with me?

I didn't grow up with the tradition of Advent. One December, when our children were younger we participated in our church's Advent services. We lit candles, one each week, and shared thoughts on Hope, Peace, Joy and Love. It became a beautiful, meaningful tradition for our family, one we chose to continue in our home each year.

Sometimes our traditions become just that -- traditions. Actions and words whose living meaning and life changing value have been set aside, replaced by duty or necessity, grown cold and misunderstood with seasons and age.

It's time to pick them up again.

Advent literally means: **The coming or arrival, especially of something extremely important.** It's time to look to the coming of Emmanuel and what it means for transforming our lives and fulfilling a plan of redemption that began in a stable.

It's time to journey to Bethlehem!

What will our footprints look like? How will we be released from hopelessness, unrest, sorrow, and loneliness, into hope, peace, joy and love? As we journey to Bethlehem together, can we invite Emmanuel, our redeeming, compassionate God, to transform our story and illuminate our lives?

Imagine we're traveling together to Bethlehem, each carrying a light. Older ones helping the younger, in expectation of Emmanuel's coming. I'm envisioning a ribbon of light, the illumination of God's redeeming, transforming work in our lives, and I am hearing the words of Isaiah:

"The people who walk in darkness will see a great light. For those who live in a land of deep darkness, a light will shine. You will enlarge the nation of Israel, and its people will rejoice. They will rejoice before you as people rejoice at the harvest and like warriors dividing the plunder. For you will break the yoke of their slavery and lift the heavy burden from their shoulders. You will break the oppressor's rod, just as you did when you destroyed the army of Midian.

For a child is born to us, a son is given to us. The government will rest on his shoulders. And he will be called: Wonderful, Counsellor, Mighty God, Everlasting Father, Prince of Peace. His government and its peace will never end. He will rule with fairness and justice from the throne of his ancestor David for all eternity. The passionate commitment of the Lord of Heaven's Armies will make this happen!"

(Isaiah 9.2-7)

Each Sunday in the four weeks leading to Christmas, you will have the opportunity to light a candle for that week. (See Appendix Two for yearly dates.) There will also be a candle to light on Christmas Eve/Day. For some of you, this will mean traditional pink, purple, and white candles on an advent wreath. (These can be purchased at most Christian retail or craft stores.) For others, it may be five candles, set out on your table in the colours and containers of your choice. The importance of the celebration is that it reflects who you are as individuals/families. Be creative!

On the Sunday of each week, there is a reading to accompany the candle lighting, as well as a carol that helps carry the theme for the week. The remaining days of the week have scripture, stories, reflections, and thoughts to help us leave footprints in the themes and turn our hearts to the greatest gift we've ever been given.

In Appendix One, you will find an interactive candle lighting script for families with young children. It was written so that our children could actively participate in the candle lighting, rather than just listening. Again, doing what represents you, your family, and your journey together is what's important!

~Hope~   ~Peace~   ~Joy~   ~Love~

Traditionally the candles are
1: Prophecy or Hope Candle (purple);
2: Bethlehem or Peace Candle (purple);
3: Angel or Joy candle (pink);
4: Shepherd or Love candle (purple);
5: Christ Candle (white)

When your heart is stirred to hold on to His promises this advent, it will bring **Hope**...light the candle.

When you are allowed into someone's story there will be thankfulness and **Peace**...light the candle.

When the burden is lifted from your shoulders there will be freedom and great **Joy**...light the candle.

When the greatest **Love** of all transforms your life this advent...light the candle.

It will remind you of the promise that people who walk in darkness will see a great light. For those who live in a land of deep darkness, a light will shine. Let's journey to Bethlehem this advent, a luminous ribbon of seeking, anticipating hearts. Of all the lights that will shine this season, this is the one I want to remember!

Week One:
Leaving Footprints
in Hope

Sunday

Scripture reading:

Isaiah 9:2-7

The Prophecy/Hope Candle

Long ago in the times of the Old Testament, God spoke to His people, Israel. God spoke in many, different times and places and in different ways. God always spoke through His prophets.

The prophets were people who did two things: They listened and they spoke. They listened to God. He told them His heart, His plan. The things His people needed to hear.

The prophets conveyed the message when God was angry and grieved at the sin, and when there were going to be consequences. They told the people not to be sad or afraid.

God still loved them, had not forgotten about them. He was still their God. Always. And then one day, He whispered to the prophets. A beautiful secret. A promise. And those who listened, who set their hearts to believe... they knew what God was going to do.

He would come. God among men. A Savior for the people.

The prophet Isaiah stepped forward to say that the Savior would be born and the child would be called Immanuel. And the people whispered as one voice, "God with us!" And each of the prophets repeated the promise, the words they kept hearing from heaven, "God is coming."

Then one day, God stopped speaking. The prophet Malachi was the last to utter the promise; his were the last words given to hold on to. And then there was stillness. Not for an hour, a day or a year. Four hundred years. It must have been deafening. No more prophets, or promises, just silence.

They reminded each other. Grandparents whispered the promise to grandchildren, knowing they might never see the fulfillment. Parents sat at bedsides, lulling children to sleep with the story of the Messiah. There must have been many who wept in doubt, cried out in desperation, and agonized over every word of the prophecy. Still, they waited, fanning the spark of Hope and promise.

As you light the Hope Candle, look closely at the burning flame. Remember that even during those silent years, some of God's people had a flame burning in their hearts that could not be extinguished. A flame of faith. They never stopped believing the old, old prophecies about the coming of Immanuel. A flame of Hope. One day, He would break the silence. The waiting would be over, He would come.

Wherever you are waiting today, whatever your heart longs for, hold on to Hope. God will be faithful. He can be trusted to keep His promise.

O Come, O Come Emmanuel
O come, O come Immanuel!
And ransom captive Israel.
Who mourns in lonely exile here,
Until the son of God appears.
Rejoice! Rejoice!
Immanuel shall come to thee O Israel

O come, Thou Key of David, come,
And open wide our heavenly home;
Make safe the way that leads on high,
And close the path to misery.
Rejoice! Rejoice!
Immanuel shall come to thee, O Israel.

Leaving Footprints in Hope
Monday:
Luke 1:1-6

"Many have undertaken to draw up an account of the things that have been fulfilled among us, just as they were handed down to us by those who from the first were eyewitnesses and servants of the word. With this in mind, since I myself have carefully investigated everything from the beginning, I too decided to write an orderly account for you, most excellent Theophilus, so that you may know the certainty of the things you have been taught. In the time of Herod king of Judea there was a priest named Zechariah, who belonged to the priestly division of Abijah; his wife Elizabeth was also a descendant of Aaron. Both of them were righteous in the sight of God, observing all the Lord's commands and decrees blamelessly."

Of Gifts and Giving

Candles, small bottles of lotion, brightly coloured ornaments and stationary lined the desk top. All of the teacher's gifts had been opened, and now the students were preparing to go home for the holidays. Cold wind swept down the hall, and excited voices echoed off the walls. Only one child stood at the corner of the desk. Scrubbing the floor with the toe of her shoe, she bit her lip and whispered, "I wanted to get you something." The teacher glanced at the display on the desk, and felt her heart constrict for the little girl who wanted to give but couldn't.

"There is one thing you could give me," she said. The child's head jerked up and her eyes grew wide, as the teacher continued. "The best gift I could have would be a big hug from you."

"Really?" The little girl shifted feet and a smile played on her lips.

"Really," said her teacher.

With a laugh, the little girl ran full force into the teacher's arms and gave her a tight hug. Tugging on her mittens, she reached the door, ready to join the laughing group of children in the hall. Her face grew thoughtful as she looked back at the teacher with a sigh. Her eyes revealed sadness beyond her years. Shaking her head she whispered "It's not enough."

~ ~ ~

It's time to start our journey, to begin to walk towards Bethlehem, celebrating the greatest gift to ever grace this planet. It's time to put our hand with the God of the universe, and discover new paths in Hope, Peace, Joy and Love. All you need to bring is you. **You are enough**. God's not looking for extravagant gifts, well-planned lists, or perfect wrapping. He loves your company, just as you are. His favorite gift is our relationship with Him. It's a safe place to give and receive Love. Let's start by running into His arms, open, expectant, and full of Grace!

It is enough.

"May our Lord Jesus Christ himself and God our Father, who loved us and by his grace gave us eternal encouragement and good hope, encourage your hearts and strengthen you in every good deed and word."

(2 Thessalonians 2:17-17)

Leaving footprints in Hope
Tuesday:
Luke 1:6-12

"But they were childless because Elizabeth was not able to conceive, and they were both very old. Once when Zechariah's division was on duty and he was serving as priest before God, he was chosen by lot, according to the custom of the priesthood, to go into the temple of the Lord and burn incense. And when the time for the burning of incense came, all the assembled worshipers were praying outside. Then an angel of the Lord appeared to him, standing at the right side of the altar of incense. When Zechariah saw him, he was startled and was gripped with fear."

Turkeys and Expectations

I won't ever forget that Christmas morning. I was up early, tree lights twinkling, coffee brewing and a large eighteen pound turkey waiting to be stuffed! I pulled the bird out of the fridge where it had been thawing, and set it on the counter. There are only six of us, but my motto has always been that if you are going to cook a turkey, it might as well be a big one, and then there will be lots of leftovers!

Much of the preparation had been done the day before in anticipation of an afternoon filled with board games and reading, while the smell of roasting turkey filled the air! I set out my biggest roasting pan, and began to un-wrap the bird. I thought at first it might be the pan, or something in the sink. Had someone left the organics bin open? My growing sense of apprehension turned into a full blown groan of reality when I put my nose closer to the turkey and sniffed... it was bad!

Where was I going to find another turkey? Every store was closed! It all disappeared with one whiff. The smell of turkey filling the house, a beautiful brown bird on the table, all the wonderful meals I was planning for the leftovers! All my expectations for a perfect Christmas dinner were sent out with the trash. I was upset, to put it mildly, and I was the only one. The kids thought having chicken fingers with their mashed potatoes was great! We still had a fun-filled afternoon, savouring our time together.

Those expectations, where did they come from? Obviously not from the group at the table enjoying chicken fingers! I had picked up those expectations from somewhere and put them on myself! Since then, I've learned to ask myself some "expectation questions" when the holiday season comes around.

What are we hoping for and why? What are our expectations and where do they come from? If they are rooted in pride, perfectionism, or worth, or if they are put on us by others... it's time to let them go! The God of the universe is so willing to take them, and replace them with Grace, Hope, and all-encompassing love!

*"But now, Lord, what do I look for?
My hope is in you."*

(Psalm 39:7)

Leaving Footprints in Hope
Wednesday:
Luke 1:13-17

"But the angel said to him: 'Do not be afraid, Zechariah; your prayer has been heard. Your wife Elizabeth will bear you a son, and you are to call him John. He will be a joy and delight to you, and many will rejoice because of his birth, for he will be great in the sight of the Lord. He is never to take wine or other fermented drink, and he will be filled with the Holy Spirit even before he is born. He will bring back many of the people of Israel to the Lord their God. And he will go on before the Lord, in the spirit and power of Elijah, to turn the hearts of the parents to their children and the disobedient to the wisdom of the righteous—to make ready a people prepared for the Lord.'"

Canned Sweet Yams

It was a grocery store, not unlike thousands of other supermarket chains across the country. The neon sign, lit up even in the day, proclaimed it was the best place to shop for value. There are no distinctions in a grocery store. All races, rich, poor, homeless, well or sick; anyone who steps on the automatic doormat is instantly welcomed. On a given day you will find any or all of the above, rubbing elbows in the produce aisle. And each of them has a story...

On this particular day it was busier than usual, due in part, to the fact that the radio had begun announcing the days left until Christmas. They seemed to start earlier every year, whipping the general public into a complete frenzy. Otherwise logical shoppers began believing that it was a catastrophe of huge proportions if they had not purchased the fixings for an entire Christmas celebration by November the 10th.

As is often the case, there were too few cashiers and long lines that stretched back across the main aisle, making it almost impossible for a shopper with a full cart to negotiate the front of the store. The express checkout, with the "8-12 Items" sign had a line that stretched back to the meat department. Several carts were obviously carrying more than the limit, and their owners wore a look that said either, "I hope I can get through with these items," or, "I dare anyone to try and stop me."

Overhead, the PA system blasted a poor rendition of "Silver Bells" followed by "I'll Be Home for Christmas." Not to be outdone by the music, the lotto machine at the customer service counter chimed away, printing and checking tickets for hopeful customers. A woman in a faded blue jacket handed the clerk a handful of bills and said, "Maybe I'll win enough to have a real good Christmas this year." She laughed, a tired laugh as faded as her jacket. "I hope so," she said softly as she took her tickets.

"I hope so too," said the clerk flatly. Looking up from her till she yelled, "Next!"

The lines moved slowly and every time the bell clanged for a price check there was an audible groan from the crowd. The grainy music droned on into "Winter Wonderland"

and "Frosty." It seemed as if we had been waiting forever, but the clock on the wall said only five minutes had passed.

Ring, ring...another price check...another groan. The beep, beep, beep of the scanners was loud, and visibly annoying to the well-dressed woman who was now third in line. She was trying to talk on a cell phone, and could not be heard. Raising her voice she repeated, "I'm at the store. I've been waiting for at least half an hour. They're so slow here. I hope I can make it in time." She snapped her phone shut, just as the little boy waiting behind her tugged on her coat.

"Lady, is this your button?" he asked with a grin. Realizing it had indeed come from her coat, she snatched it from his sticky hand, and with a look of distain turned to face the front of the line.

"I hope you can glue it on," he said to the back of the tall form in front of him. But there was no reply.

A baby in lane 3 cried incessantly, cell phones rang, and the homeless man who comes in for the complimentary coffee was repeating, "Please to meet you," over and over.

Two older women in lane five were oblivious to the rest of the room. They had gone to school together 40, or was it 45, years ago now? They had lost touch and always hoped to see each other again. What a wonderful surprise! Could they get together over the holidays? They hoped so. They were rummaging in purses for paper to write down phone numbers.

Two more customers and then it was my turn. Did I really need this butter? Had I also bought into some large conspiracy by believing that my shortbread had to be finished today? I sighed and groaned with everyone else at the infernal dinging of the price check bell.

We were tired of waiting, tired of hoping that the line would move quickly or that the manager would send out a flock of new cashiers. Patience was growing thin and tempers were flaring. "Please to meet you, please to meet you." beep, beep, beep. The PA had switched to a Sacred Christmas track, and "O Come, O come Emanuel" spilled out over the crowd.

Behind me, at the end of aisle three, was a display of canned sweet yams: 59 cents a tin. That's a bargain any time of the year and a gold mine in mid-November! The shelf was empty except for one solitary tin. One tin, two outstretched hands and no patience, equals an argument. "O Come O come Emanuel" is interrupted by the announcement, "Manager to aisle three."

In front of me a girl of five or six flashed me a bright smile. Her pigtails bounced as she twirled some freestyle dance steps in the limited space between carts. Her dad was anxiously scanning his cart, mentally adding up the cost of the items.

"Do you have enough, Daddy?" she asked between dance steps.

"Let's hope," he murmured.

"Can I sing you a song?" she asked him.

"Uh huh," was his absentminded answer.

What happened next would forever change the Value Mart, at least for me. Its sliding doors would ever after open to holy ground. It was a place where, for a moment in time, heaven touched earth to remind us that in the waiting there is Love. And because of Love, there is Hope; a hope of something far, far greater.

Standing as tall as any six year old can, the little girl who danced opened her mouth and began to sing in a loud clear voice:

**"Away in a manger, no crib for a bed, the little Lord Jesus lay down his sweet head.
The stars in the bright sky looked down where he lay, the little Lord Jesus, asleep on the hay."**

Her father stopped his mental calculations and smiled at his daughter. Sheepishly he glanced around at the rest of us. But all eyes were focussed on her. Ignoring the crowd she was spurred on by her Dad's smile and began the second verse...

"The cattle are lowing the baby awakes ..."

As if on cue, the baby in lane three began its wailing again, drowning out some of the verse before his mother replaced his soother.

"I love you Lord Jesus, look down from the sky.
And stay by my bedside till morning is nigh."

The sounds and frustrations of our waiting were secondary now as we focussed on the dancer's song.

"Be near me Lord Jesus ..."

"He is here," I thought as I glanced around. The reunion ladies in lane five have stopped, to listen to the little messenger.

"I ask you to stay, close by me forever and Love me I pray ..."

Love me; whether I am rich or poor, old or young, homeless, sick or well...

"Bless all the dear children in your tender care ..."

"We are all your children," I whispered, "surrounded by your love, whether we see it or not." Sometimes we need an angel to just stand up and remind us.

"And take us to heaven to live with you there."

Ah! Hope, because of God's Love.

"Was that good Daddy? It's for our concert. I learned it at Sunday School. My teacher says..." The dancer's explanation is cut short by a tin rolling across the floor and landing at her feet.

"Daddy, look! It's one of them sale cans of yams. The ones we couldn't find. We can put the other can back and then we'll have enough, right?"

Embarrassed, the man looked for the owner of the can, one of the women in the argument with the manager. His daughter, unaware of her impact on this crowd, continued, looking straight up at the manager.

"We're havin' Christmas early this year 'cause my grandpa is going to heaven, and we want to have a nice dinner before he goes."

There should have been a bright light, a celestial chorus, something to mark the impact of this event in time and space. But there was only the hum of a crowd, a muffled version of "O Little Town of Bethlehem," and the steady beep, beep, beep of the registers.

I'm not sure where the arguing ladies went. After putting the tin of yams in the man's cart, the manager walked to the back, wiping his eyes as he went. The PA was grinding out "Joy to the World," and then it was my turn to check out. Beep. Fifteen minutes of waiting in line. Is it possible to be so utterly changed in fifteen minutes? The reunion ladies were embracing by the payphone. Homeless Jim has moved to a bench near the sliding door.

"Please to meet you, please to meet you. Please to meet you".

"Who did you meet Jim?" I wondered as I unlocked my car door. Was it Emmanuel? He was in the Value Mart today, loving us, and speaking a message of Hope into our lives. The lost, the found, the seeking, and the faded. The wounded, the innocent, the hurt, the healed, the joyful and the dancers. He came for us all... and everyone has a story.

"He who did not spare his own Son, but gave him up for us all..."

(Romans 8:32)

Leaving Footprints in Hope
Thursday:
Luke 1:18-20

"*Zechariah asked the angel, 'How can I be sure of this? I am an old man and my wife is well along in years.' The angel said to him, 'I am Gabriel. I stand in the presence of God, and I have been sent to speak to you and to tell you this good news. And now you will be silent and not able to speak until the day this happens, because you did not believe my words, which will come true at their appointed time.'*"

The Scent of Hope

When the smell of ginger and molasses cookies wafts through the house, everyone knows: **It's time for Christmas.** It's a tradition, and if nothing else gets baked, these cookies do. I think it's the combination of fragrant spices and the warm simplicity that make these one of our favorites. While I inhale the perfume of the season, I think about hope and promise.

This birth, the coming of Christ, was only the beginning. Soon, the baby would grow to be the man hanging between two thieves on a wind-swept hill. There would be a living, breathing man on earth who would show us that living in relationship with the God of the universe was real and He would die to make it possible.

There would be spices then too, but not in celebration. They would be brought for burial, mingled with the tears of women who came to anoint the body. In the midst of grief and despair, there was hope. It surrounded them with every stir of perfumed, scented air, and it culminated in the resurrection! He kept his word. The desire of His heart from before time would be fulfilled, no matter what it may have looked like. Wherever we stand today, whatever it looks like... He is stirring the winds, heavy with the fragrance of Hope, and He will keep His word.

"You are my refuge and my shield; I have put my hope in your word."
(Psalm 119:114)

Ginger Molasses Cookies

1 c. sugar
¼ c. molasses
1 Egg
3/4 c. butter, melted
Mix together:
2 c. flour
2 tsp. baking soda
1/2 tsp. salt
1 heaping tsp. cinnamon
1/2 tsp. ginger
1/2 tsp. cloves
1/4 tsp. Nutmeg

Add the sugar to the molasses. Add the egg. Gradually add melted butter and flour mixture to sugar mix. Roll dough between hands into ball size about 3/4 inch. Roll in granulated sugar (I think organic sugar makes them sparkle more, maybe because it's course) and place on a greased cookie sheet. Bake at 375 degrees for about 8 to 10 minutes.

Leaving Footprints in Hope
Friday:
Luke 1:21-25

"Meanwhile, the people were waiting for Zechariah and wondering why he stayed so long in the temple. When he came out, he could not speak to them. They realized he had seen a vision in the temple, for he kept making signs to them but remained unable to speak. When his time of service was completed, he returned home. After this his wife Elizabeth became pregnant and for five months he remained in seclusion. 'The Lord has done this for me,' she said. 'In these days he has shown his favor and taken away my disgrace among the people.'"

In The Waiting...

My children's hands were small, the first time they opened the surprise. They sat together at the kitchen table, heads bent in earnest. Little fingers impatiently tugging at tiny cardboard flaps. They had been waiting for the first day of December, gazing at the brightly coloured calendars and dreaming of the things that lay behind the numbered doors.

Advent Calendars!

All four of them waited each day, for me to reach up to the safety of the shelf and place those cardboard treasures into their outstretched arms. Finally, smiles spread across faces as they tasted the sweetness of surprise, and chocolate! And so it went, onward through December, until there were only empty cartons... and the anticipation of next year!

Little hands grew big, and yet every year they still receive a calendar! They don't wait for me to hand it to them anymore. They don't need to. The shelf is well within their reach now and I have to stand tiptoe to hug them! Some years, a couple of them have laughingly skipped the daily routine and emptied the doors, all of them in one sitting. No waiting that year! The result was fun, although brief, and in the days that followed, they learned that siblings will not share when it comes to the Advent calendar!

~~~

Waiting is never easy. Whether it's a good, hope-filled waiting, or waiting in sadness, it's made easier with the company of others. Hope is upheld. There is encouragement, shared longing, and understanding. Sharing anticipation, excitement, and surprise is so much sweeter when others are walking with you. It's in community, no matter the size, that we can discover that in the waiting there is hope, and in the hoping - Love. This amazing journey we are travelling was never meant to be walked alone.

Who are you waiting and walking with today? What would encouragement look like this week for those who journey with you?

"But you, dear friends, by building yourselves up in your most holy faith and praying in the Holy Spirit, keep

yourselves in God's love as you wait for the mercy of our Lord Jesus Christ to bring you to eternal life."

(Jude 1:20-21)

Leaving Footprints in Hope

Saturday:

Luke 1:26-28

"In the sixth month of Elizabeth's pregnancy, God sent the angel Gabriel to Nazareth, a town in Galilee, to a virgin pledged to be married to a man named Joseph, a descendant of David. The virgin's name was Mary. The angel went to her and said, 'Greetings, you who are highly favored! The Lord is with you.'"

Mary

Mary's sandals scuffed the dirt and kept perfect time with the beating of her heart. Dust swirled upwards on a warm breeze that carried the greetings of neighbors and friends. Everything seemed the same. A water jug at her side, she travelled the well-rutted roads as if it were any other day. It wasn't. Breathing deep to steady her pulse, she focused on the path ahead, and the fragrant vineyards that surrounded her.

On the outside she smiled and greeted the neighbors; on the inside - she carried new life. The son of God, that's what the angel had said. She knew the prophecy, she'd heard it spoken often, but never in her wildest dreams did she imagine she would be part of the fulfillment. God, growing in her, here in Nazareth; how could it be?

Bending down to fill her jug, she listened to the splashing water, filling it to over- flowing.

A laugh escaped her lips before she had a chance to stop it, and she marvelled at the thought. The Messiah, filling her, just as the water filled the jar!

The Hope that had been carried, passed down, clung to and cradled - had found a resting place. The weight of the water slowed her steps, and gave her time to ponder this expected life that would change everything. The shade of an olive tree cast a momentary shadow, and water from the full jug trickled to the ground.

Love had come for the thirsty hearts of the people. It began in the heart of the Godhead, filling the girl from Nazareth, and one day in the shadow of another tree, it would be poured out for all.

"She will give birth to a son, and you are to give him the name Jesus, because he will save his people from their sins."
(Matthew 1:21)

Week Two:
Leaving Footprints
in Peace

Sunday

Scripture Reading: Matthew 2:5-6

The Bethlehem/Peace Candle

The prophets promised there would be a Savior whose name would be Immanuel, "God with us." Four hundred long years God's people hoped, and waited through the silence. All the while, they were holding on to the promise. God's promise.

Perhaps around the table they reminded each other, God always keeps his promises. And maybe in the dim light of evening they wondered how the promise would be fulfilled.

Would the Messiah come to the biggest city, or the grandest temple? Would there be lavish celebrations, a sweeping entry of the one who would save them? In all of their wildest dreams, did anyone imagine...

Bethlehem?

The little town where Jesus was born.

Bethlehem, which means "house of bread."

A small ordinary town, filled with ordinary people.

Given the chance to choose, would any of us have chosen Bethlehem? This was Immanuel. He was the promised savior of the world, God's chosen one! Our thoughts would have turned to the biggest, brightest, the most extravagant and extraordinary.

But, His thoughts are not ours.

Little Bethlehem would welcome the bread of life.

The King of Kings and Lord of Lords would enter our world in a cave, hewn from the rock in the side of a hill. Stark and insignificant, surrounded by barn animals. Not by accident or haphazard chance. It was by choice, and it was all about love.

He always keeps His promises, and sometimes it's not what we expect.

As you light the Bethlehem Candle, hold tight to this: God kept the promise He made through the prophets. In all of the waiting, darkness and silence, there was hope. Out of a heart of unimaginable Love, came a plan and a promise, far greater than we could ever imagine. In a small, nondescript city, a great light shone.   Jesus was born in Bethlehem.

God ALWAYS keeps His promises. They may not be kept the way we expect them to be. Our God thinks differently than we do. His heart overflows with plans and purpose and they are good! Whatever the promise, the waiting, the hoping today, remember the stable. He always keeps His promises, sourced in Love and overflowing with unexpected peace and grace!

O Little Town of Bethlehem
O little town of Bethlehem,
How still we see thee lie,
Above thy deep and dreamless sleep,
The silent stars go by.
Yet in thy dark street shineth
The everlasting light.
The hopes and fears of all the years
Are met in thee tonight.

How silently, how silently,
The wondrous gift is given.
So God imparts to human hearts
The wonders of His heaven
No ear may hear his calling,
Yet in this world of sin,
Where meek souls will receive Him still,
The dear Christ enters in.

Leaving Footprints in Peace

Monday:

Luke 1:29-33

"Mary was greatly troubled at his words and wondered what kind of greeting this might be. But the angel said to her, 'Do not be afraid, Mary; you have found favor with God. You will conceive and give birth to a son, and you are to call him Jesus. He will be great and will be called the Son of the Most High. The Lord God will give him the throne of his father David, and he will reign over Jacob's descendants forever; his kingdom will never end.'"

Simply a Christmas Tree

It stands in the corner of our living room, silently. It took us all evening to choose. We checked for a straight trunk, full branches and a lovely green color. And now it will wait until we have the time to string lights inside the boughs, and hang ornaments from the tips of its graceful branches. We could do it right away, but we're never in a hurry, because it's beautiful as it is. Without the weight of decorations, it's breathtaking in its real, authentic state.

I like a day or two of admiration, moments to breathe in the perfume of pine. The simple, bare branches offer the chance to marvel at pine needles in intricate patterns and vivid shades of green. It's the simplicity of it, the uncomplicated, uncovered beauty. I enjoy the lights and decorations, but I sometimes wonder what it would be like to leave it just like it is, for the season.

Real, Honest, Open and De-cluttered.

While I fill the stand with water, I contemplate a Christmas season and then a life, lived within the framework of those words.

True, Authentic, and Free.

There has to be a letting go of all the things that cover up and complicate. And this is the great gift of Grace: With unending Love, the God of the universe lifts off all those things we carry and uncovers the real, beautiful and honest in our lives. He patiently removes the weight of life's clutter, stripping away the things that hide the amazing, intricate design of who He created us to be!

"I praise you because I am fearfully and wonderfully made; your works are wonderful, I know that full well."
(Psalm 149:13)

Leaving Footprints in Peace
Tuesday:
Luke 1:34- 38

"'How will this be,' Mary asked the angel, 'since I am a virgin?' The angel answered, 'The Holy Spirit will come on you, and the power of the Most High will overshadow you. So the holy one to be born, will be called the Son of God. Even Elizabeth your relative is going to have a child in her old age, and she who was said to be unable to conceive is in her sixth month. For no word from God will ever fail.' 'I am the Lord's servant,' Mary answered. 'May your word to me be fulfilled.' Then the angel left her."

I heard the bells on Christmas day,
Their old familiar carols play,
And wild and sweet the words repeat,
Of peace on earth, good will to men.

And thought how, as the day had come,
The belfries of all Christendom
Had rolled along the unbroken song,
Of peace on earth, good will to men.

Till ringing, singing on its way,
The world revolved from night to day,
A voice, a chime, a chant sublime,
Of peace on earth, good will to men.

And in despair I bowed my head,
"There is no peace on earth," I said,
"For hate is strong and mocks the song,
Of peace on earth, good will to men."

Then pealed the bells more loud and deep:
"God is not dead, nor doth He sleep;
The wrong shall fail, the right prevail,
With peace on earth, good will to men."

The Sound of Peace

This beautiful carol was originally a poem, penned by Henry Wadsworth Longfellow in 1864. It was written three years after the tragic loss of his wife in an accident, and the crippling injury of his son, who was fighting in the Civil war. Each Christmas following the accidents, his journal entries reflected hopelessness, the feeling that peace and happiness could no longer be part of his life. There is no entry for Christmas 1863, only silence.

On Christmas day in 1864, while the Civil war still raged, he sat down and wrote what was originally called "Christmas Bells." The war would not see an end for several months, and his circumstances had not changed, but this bit of light shone into his dark place:

Peace does not depend on the circumstances around us.

So much of the turmoil in our world is difficult to understand. In all of the unrest that often swirls around us, this truth can be grasped and held tight;

God is, and will always be, living and present with us... Emmanuel.

He is our Peace.

"For unto us a Child is born, unto us a Son is given: and the government shall be upon His shoulder: and His Name shall be called Wonderful, Counsellor, The Mighty God, The Everlasting Father, The Prince of Peace."

(Isaiah 9:6)

Leaving Footprints in Peace

Wednesday:

Luke 1:39-41

"At that time Mary got ready and hurried to a town in the hill country of Judea, where she entered Zechariah's home and greeted Elizabeth. When Elizabeth heard Mary's greeting, the baby leaped in her womb, and Elizabeth was filled with the Holy Spirit."

That Place of Peace

I wrap cold hands around a warm coffee mug. The wind whistling just outside the window is the only sound this late at night. The silence of sleep has settled in like the snow on the front lawn, and I'm the only one left to keep company with the night. These moments that only come around once a year, need to be savoured.

Wrapped in the warmth of a blanket, I bask in the glow of tiny twinkling lights. They take center stage. All the carefully hung ornaments fade into the background. The deep majestic pine in the corner of the dark living room becomes a canvas, not unlike the night sky, where handfuls of starry light have been flung.

I squint, watching the light bend and twist, and my heart settles into that place of peace. Everything before this quiet moment in time is now part of the rear view, and everything beyond this time of late night Christmas contemplation is yet unseen. Worship and gratitude spill out into the night as I give thanks for the one who is with me in the seen and the unseen, always, Emmanuel.

I prop up two more pillows, and I wonder what it was like for her, Mary. Did her makeshift bed of straw and blankets give her a view of the night sky? Did she squint at the multitudes of stars, unusually bright, hanging on the canvas just outside the cave? While she cradled the son of God, did her heart settle into that place of peace?

Everything before that first lusty, newborn cry was now part of the rear view, and everything beyond savouring the sweet rest of that moment was yet unseen. Even before the shepherds' arrival, I imagine worship and gratitude filled every corner of that stable as she gave thanks that He was there, her Emmanuel.

The last bit of coffee in the mug has gone cold, but Grace covers me, warmer than the blankets I've wrapped tight. Long after the tree lights have been extinguished, this truth will forever illuminate the canvas of our lives; Emmanuel is God with us. Always. Walking with us in thankfulness, worship and peace.

"The Lord gives strength to his people; the Lord blesses his people with peace."

(Psalm 29:11)

Leaving Footprints in Peace

Thursday:

Luke 1:42-45

"In a loud voice she exclaimed: 'Blessed are you among women, and blessed is the child you will bear! But why am I so favored, that the mother of my Lord should come to me? As soon as the sound of your greeting reached my ears, the baby in my womb leaped for joy. Blessed is she who has believed that the Lord would fulfill his promises to her!'"

Thumbprints

"I want to use my own fumb," she cried, in a burst of two year old independence. I watched while she pressed her little thumb into waiting balls of dough, lined up like sentinels on the cookie sheet. We were wearing Christmas aprons. Hers reached almost to her toes, and mine was covering the bump which cradled her soon-to-arrive baby sister. Her enthusiasm lasted for half a row more, and then she was off to explore the wonders of her toy box. I finished the rows with my own thumbprint, and baked them while she napped.

At the end of the afternoon, rows of freshly baked cookies lined the counter. Each indented bit of crispy, golden-brown goodness was filled with festive strawberry jam. Some were coated with nuts, the rest were plain. It was easy to see which ones were created by my daughter. Her small thumb had left only a small well for the jam, compared to my larger one. She was quick to proudly point out to her dad, which ones belonged to her!

How often we forget who we belong to. The same God the angels praised when they announced the birth of Christ has placed His thumbprint in us! The God that flung the stars in space, and arranged pine tree needles in perfect patterns, is proud to point out that we belong to Him! He created, formed and loved us, before we ever drew breath. We're sons and daughters of an amazing God, and He is delighted with who He created us to be. Nutty or plain, it makes no difference. We are His and we are loved. And that indent? It's the perfect size and shape for the spirit that fills us, and gives us life!

"But now, this is what the Lord says— he who created you, Jacob, he who formed you, Israel: *"Do not fear, for I have redeemed you; I have summoned you by name; you are mine."*

(Isaiah 43:1)

Christmas Thumbprint Cookies

2 cups unsalted butter
1 cup packed brown sugar
4 eggs
2 teaspoons vanilla extract
1/4 teaspoon salt
4 cups all-purpose flour
1/2 cup strawberry/or other fruit jam
2 cups finely chopped walnuts

Preheat oven to 350 degrees F (175 degrees C).

Beat butter and sugar in large bowl at low speed until mixture becomes fluffy. Separate the eggs and beat in egg yolks, vanilla and salt until blended. Add flour all at once. Beat at low speed, scraping side of bowl often, 2 minutes or until well mixed.

Beat egg whites, slightly.

Roll dough into 1 inch balls and dip each ball into egg whites. Roll in nuts if desired. Place about 1 inch apart on greased sheets. Make a depression in center of each cookie with thumb.

Bake for about 10 minutes or until light brown. Cool on wire rack. Fill with jam.

Leaving Footprints in Peace
Friday:
Luke 1:46-50

"And Mary said: 'My soul glorifies the Lord and my spirit rejoices in God my Savior, for he has been mindful of the humble state of his servant. From now on all generations will call me blessed, for the Mighty One has done great things for me— holy is his name. His mercy extends to those who fear him, from generation to generation.'"

The Christmas Card

The first Christmas card was believed to have been designed and printed in 1843. Since then a variety of styles, shapes and sizes of Christmas cards have been produced, offering a large selection of ways to pass on holiday greetings. In recent years, e-cards have also become a convenient, popular way to wish far away friends and family a Merry Christmas!

I will admit to loving a mailbox filled with brightly coloured envelopes when the season comes around again! We have displayed ours on strings stretched across a living room wall, taped them to doors, arranged stacks in holders, and placed them in festive containers.

One of my favorite things to do with the received cards was to place them in a basket on our dining room table. Once Christmas had passed and the New Year had been ushered in, we would choose one card from the basket each night at the dinner table. Along with giving thanks for the food that had been provided, we would pray for the sender of the chosen Christmas card. Names of e-card senders were printed out on slips of paper and included with the cards.

It's a wonderful way to bless friends and family, extending the warmth of the season, long into the cold winter months.

Do you have plans for the Christmas cards you will receive this year?

"I thank my God every time I remember you."

(Philippians 1:3)

Leaving Footprints in Peace

Saturday:

Luke 1:51-56

"'He has performed mighty deeds with his arm; he has scattered those who are proud in their inmost thoughts. He has brought down rulers from their thrones but has lifted up the humble. He has filled the hungry with good things but has sent the rich away empty. He has helped his servant Israel, remembering to be merciful to Abraham and his descendants forever, just as he promised our ancestors.' Mary stayed with Elizabeth for about three months and then returned home."

Joseph

The hammer slammed into the wood, unusually hard, and overly loud. Again and again he drove the hammer against the half-finished yoke. The goats just beginning to graze outside the shed scattered. Dropping the tool in the basket, he leaned on the rough boards of the table, and cradled his head. Only the yoke and an old saw heard the whispered words "Why me?"

He'd stumbled down the path in the dark and the new day was only now beginning to pierce the night. He hadn't known where else to go, after a dream woke him from a deep sleep and left him shaken. The pale light of dawn slipped in the window, and underneath the door.

Joseph reached for the stool and, sighing deeply, let his full weight rest on it. He had planned it all, worked out the details. It would have been a quiet divorce, the best he could have done given the law, because he loved her. His Mary. The one he'd chosen to share life with. He had spent many evenings planning and dreaming of their life together, but that was before she'd told him what the angel had said. He had wanted to believe her. He knew the talk that swirled around the well and out by the wine press, but he knew her, his Mary. His heart had shattered, and fear had crept into all the broken places. Still, she'd been so confident, and clear, he'd wanted to believe, and now he did.

Last night's dream had erased the doubt. The fear that threatened to overwhelm him was swallowed up in the angel's words. It was not fear that kept him here, wrestling with wood at dawn. It was the gnawing realization that he was going to be a father to the son of God. How could this be possible, and why would God choose him? There must be others far more qualified than he!

It was lighter now, and the village was beginning to stir. Joseph looked down at his hands, rough and calloused from working with stone and wood. It was all he had to offer. Opening his hands, he spread them on the table and whispered to the dawn.

"God of our Fathers, I will do as you have spoken, blessed be your name."

The morning sun entered the shed along with peace, and Joseph left to find Mary. Together they would begin a journey that would start with a baby and culminate with another pair of outstretched hands, and the rough-hewn wood of a cross.

Week Three: Leaving Footprints in Joy

Sunday

Scripture Reading

Nehemiah 8:10

The Shepherd's/ Joy Candle

It began with the promise. A promise made through the Old Testament prophets. Despite years of silence and waiting, God kept His promise. God the Eternal Son came to earth and was born as a tiny baby. Immanuel was born in a barn, in the small, unimportant town of Bethlehem. It was the most incredible and amazing event that had ever occurred. The invisible God had become a human being!

And there was hardly anyone there to witness it. Only Mary, Joseph, and a few animals. I wonder if the new parents who huddled together in the cave, thought it was meant to be a secret. A cry in the dark on the hillside of Bethlehem was only the beginning of the announcement.

God had a plan. This wasn't a "wait and see what happens" event. His heart had purpose, and so the good news of Jesus' birth was announced by heaven's messengers. Two very different kinds of people received the news, and it wasn't by accident.

The first was a group of shepherds who were sleeping outside with the flocks. They were Jewish people, who knew the Old Testament stories and were waiting for Immanuel. The smell of the earth and the animals they tended clung to them, branding them poor and unpopular. This was who the angels visited, bringing news of great joy. A few hours later these same shepherds were face down in a small cave, worshipping God and gazing in wonder at a baby wrapped in rags, and lying in a manger!

And that was only the beginning of the divine announcement!

There were wise men. They probably knew very little about the Old Testament, the prophets, or Immanuel and they weren't Jewish. Some of them were kings. Their lifestyle and clothing branded them as rich, respected and popular. The joyful news was announced to them by way of a brilliant star in the eastern sky. Months or possibly years later, these same wise men were bowing low, worshipping God and offering gifts of gold and expensive perfume to a new born King.

As you light the Shepherd's Candle, remember that Jesus came to earth to be the Light of the *whole* world. No matter what country you may live in or what language you may speak, Jesus was born to be your Savior. When we meet with Him we are all the same. We may be Jewish or non-Jewish, far or near, rich or poor, kings or slaves, shepherds or wise men. When we come to Jesus, those things fade away and we all become the same thing: worshipers who have come to adore Him.

O Come All Ye Faithful
O come all ye faithful,
Joyful and triumphant.
O come ye, O come ye to Bethlehem.
Come and behold Him,
Born the king of angels.
O come let us adore Him.
O come let us adore Him.
O come let us adore Him,
Christ the Lord.

Yea Lord we greet Thee,
Born this happy morning.
Jesus to Thee be all glory giv'n.
Word of the Father
Now in flesh appearing.

O come let us adore Him.
O come let us adore Him.
O come let us adore Him,
Christ the Lord.

Leaving footprints in Joy
Monday:
Luke 1: 57-58

"When it was time for Elizabeth to have her baby, she gave birth to a son. Her neighbors and relatives heard that the Lord had shown her great mercy, and they shared her joy."

Delight

Much like Grace, delight is found in the everyday. It comes often in the little things.

It's in the unexpected.
Snow covered landscapes and the parcel delivery truck.
A warm breeze in December, or a meal at your door.
Gifts wrapped in silver foil, or brown paper and string.
The sparkling delight of surprise.

It's in the allowing.
A hand to hold or quiet seasons.
Gingerbread creations and messy moments
Spontaneous fun or the quiet refuge found in the pages of a good book.
The pure delight of doing nothing.

It's in the accepting.
Warm hugs and fresh snowflakes on your face.
Silence, and talking loud above the noise.
Sweeping laughter, or holding tight to mitten-clad hands.
The warm delight of comfort.

It's in the belonging.
His Presence
His Grace
His Love
Him
The complete delight of living loved.

The LORD delights in those who fear him, who put their hope in his unfailing love.

(Psalm 147:11)

Leaving Footprints in Joy
Tuesday:
Luke 1:59-61

"On the eighth day they came to circumcise the child, and they were going to name him after his father Zechariah, but his mother spoke up and said, 'No! He is to be called John.' They said to her, 'There is no one among your relatives who has that name.'"

Traditions

Our traditions can't be compared to others. They belong to us. It doesn't matter what traditions we choose, as long as they reflect who we are, what we value, and that we do it together! For example: we always have Chinese take-out on Christmas Eve. There is a story behind it, but suffice it to say - it is easy, fun and reflects us!

About five years ago, a friend sent me this story. My husband and I were so moved by it, that we decided to adopt this tradition as one of our own...

For the Man Who Hated Christmas
by Nancy W. Gavin

It's just a small, white envelope stuck among the branches of our Christmas tree. No name, no identification, no inscription. It has peeked through the branches of our tree for the past ten years or so.

It all began because my husband Mike hated Christmas--oh, not the true meaning of Christmas, but the commercial aspects of it--overspending... the frantic running around at the last minute to get a tie for Uncle Harry and the dusting powder for Grandma---the gifts given in desperation because you couldn't think of anything else. Knowing he felt this way, I decided one year to bypass the usual shirts, sweaters, ties and so forth. I reached for something special just for Mike.

The inspiration came in an unusual way. Our son Kevin, who was 12 that year, was wrestling at the junior level at the school he attended; and shortly before Christmas, there was a non-league match against a team sponsored by an inner-city church. These youngsters, dressed in sneakers so ragged that shoestrings seemed to be the only thing holding them together, presented a sharp contrast to our boys in their spiffy blue and gold uniforms and sparkling new wrestling shoes.

As the match began, I was alarmed to see that the other team was wrestling without headgear, a kind of light helmet designed to protect a wrestler's ears. It was a luxury the ragtag team obviously could not afford. Well, we ended up walloping them. We took every weight class. And as each of their boys got up from the mat, he swaggered around in his tatters with false bravado, a kind of street pride that couldn't acknowledge defeat.

Mike, seated beside me, shook his head sadly, "I wish just one of them could have won," he said. "They have a lot of potential, but losing like this could take the heart right out of them." Mike loved kids - all kids - and he knew them, having coached little league football, baseball and lacrosse. That's when the idea for his present came.

That afternoon, I went to a local sporting goods store and bought an assortment of wrestling headgear and shoes and sent them anonymously to the inner-city church. On Christmas Eve, I placed the envelope on the tree, the note inside telling Mike what I had done and that this was his gift from me. His smile was the brightest thing about Christmas that year and in succeeding years. For each Christmas, I followed the tradition-- one year sending a group of mentally handicapped youngsters to a hockey game, another year a check to a pair of elderly brothers whose home had burned to the ground the week before Christmas, and on and on. The envelope became the highlight of our Christmas. It was always the last thing opened on Christmas morning and our children, ignoring their new toys, would stand with wide-eyed anticipation as their dad lifted the envelope from the tree to reveal its contents.

As the children grew, the toys gave way to more practical presents, but the envelope never lost its allure.

The story doesn't end there. You see, we lost Mike last year due to dreaded cancer. When Christmas rolled around, I was still so wrapped in grief that I barely got the tree up. But Christmas Eve found me placing an envelope on the tree, and in the morning, it was joined by three more. Each of our children, unbeknownst to the others, had placed an envelope on the tree for their dad. The tradition has grown and someday will expand even further with our grandchildren standing to take down the envelope. Mike's spirit, like the Christmas spirit will always be with us.

(Editor's Note: This true story was originally published in the December 14, 1982 issue of Woman's Day magazine. It was the first place winner out of thousands of entries in the magazine's "My Most Moving Holiday Tradition." For more information www.whiteenvelopeproject.org.)

Every year since reading the story, there has been a white envelope in the branches of our family's Christmas tree. It has contained notes that stated:

*3 dozen pairs of warm socks have been purchased, and donated to the homeless shelter.

*Farm equipment and seeds have been purchased for families, from World Vision.

*A donation has been made to a music program for underprivileged children, (in honor of a brother who had passed away that year.)

* A donation has been made to help build wells in places without water.

This year.... will remain a secret, until the last gift has been opened on Christmas morning. That's the tradition!

What about you? What traditions reflect you, and will hold a special place in your home this Christmas?

"Keep on loving one another as brothers and sisters. Do not forget to show hospitality to strangers, for by so doing some people have shown hospitality to angels without knowing it."

(Hebrews 13:1-2)

Leaving Footprints in Joy
Wednesday:
Luke 1:62-64

"Then they made signs to his father, to find out what he would like to name the child. He asked for a writing tablet, and to everyone's astonishment he wrote, 'His name is John.' Immediately his mouth was opened and his tongue set free, and he began to speak, praising God."

Surprised By Joy

It was the last thing left in the box. I pulled back the protective tissue and smiled. A snowman, made of string and Styrofoam balls, grinned beneath a crooked black felt hat. I'd forgotten I still had this. At one time, I'd been given three! My three oldest children had formed a line and one by one, handed me three almost identical snowmen after an afternoon at the church's Christmas craft day. I'd laughed at the girl's earnest faces and expectant looks. Praising them for their fine work I placed the snow triplets on the book shelf. A glance in their direction, even on a busy day made me smile. Who knew so much joy could be found in string and bits of pipe cleaners!

One Christmas the puppy mistook one of them for a chew toy, and then there were twins. Some of the years that followed were years when grief came in with the holidays. There was only enough energy, and heart for a few simple decorations and the twins spent some of those years at the bottom of the box.

In a flurry of yearly autumn cleaning, I decided to sort through the decorations, deciding what could be thrown out or given away. A worn, cardboard container still held the snow twins, huddled together in the corner. One of them had lost a hat, and most of his string. Their crooked noses still made me smile. Sweet joyful memories floated back, a row of three girls holding their identical snowy treasures. I had packed the best looking twin in tissue, and put the boxes away again. That was years ago, and now here I was again, sorting through "stuff."

It was time to move houses, the best time to purge what we didn't want or need! I wrestled with boxes containing memories I was ready to be done with. Tired, overwhelmed but needing to finish I reached into the last box, and there it was. Who knew so much joy would come flooding back at the site of string and a crooked felt hat!

Life hands us plenty of reasons to have to sort through our "stuff." Boxes get heavy, days bring unexpected grief, and joy gets packed away in favor of the tyranny of the urgent. Unpacking's never easy, but we never do it alone. The God of the universe walks with us surprising us with joy in the midst of the tired and worn.

Wherever you walk today, take footsteps in Gratitude and Grace, expecting to be surprised by Joy!

"You make known to me the path of life; you will fill me with joy in your presence..."

(Psalm 16.11)

Leaving Footprints in Joy
Thursday:
Luke 1:65-66

"All the neighbors were filled with awe, and throughout the hill country of Judea people were talking about all these things. Everyone who heard this wondered about it, asking, 'What then is this child going to be?' For the Lord's hand was with him."

By Any Other Name

Have you ever heard of Shutty Cakes? Every Christmas I make cinnamon rolls to have for breakfast on Christmas morning. A few years ago, we were dealing with the loss of both of our mothers, and all that comes with those "first Christmases." I was completely overwhelmed and was wondering how I would get everything finished, especially the cinnamon rolls which took time to prepare! I happened to find an easier recipe and while my husband and I were walking through the grocery store, we had a conversation that went something like this:

<u>Me</u>: I want to make this new recipe for cinnamon rolls this year.

<u>Him</u>: Sounds good.

<u>Me</u>: I've always made the yeast ones from scratch, but I just can't face all of that this year.

<u>Him</u>: It will be fine.

<u>Me</u>: What if the kids don't like them?

<u>Him</u>: Well, we could tell them to "Shut up and eat them" (which was followed by laughter in the middle of the aisle because we'd **never** tell our kids that)

And then He said... we'll call them Shutty cakes! We laughed even harder, a welcome release in a difficult season!

So... that's what was on the table that year, and when they asked.... my husband replied,

They're Shutty Cakes!

We've had them every year since. They taste amazing, and are a wonderful part of our tradition. (We did eventually tell the kids the reason for the name) In the middle of trying times, and often during the holidays, the gift of laughter can be a potent medicine. It's a reminder when we're walking in places of grief, disappointment, and uncertainty. The God of the universe holds all of our moments and our days. He gifts us with joy and walks with us in peace.

Shutty Cakes

Frozen bread dough loaves (frozen loaf must be thawed enough to cut into slices) I use two loaves per pan. Cut each loaf into 10 slices.

Spray 9 x 13 pan with cooking spray. Put raisins and nuts on bottom of pan (this is optional but oh so good!) Place bread dough slices over raisins and nuts. Be sure the pieces of dough touch.

Mix 1/2 cup sugar, 1/2 cup brown sugar, and 1 tablespoon cinnamon together. Pour mixture over dough. Then pour 4 Tbsp of vanilla pudding mix (the kind you need to cook) over everything (don't use instant pudding!).

Cut one stick of butter into 20 "pats" and place one on each of the slices (use complete stick). "Tent" the pan with foil, and put in cold oven overnight.

In the morning, use a sharp knife to poke each bun (they really rise) releasing the air, and bake uncovered, in a 350 oven for 25-30 minutes.

Invert onto tray or cookie sheet.

(lower oven temperature for glass pan to 325 degrees.)

** I use the loaves when they are still partly frozen. It makes them easier to slice.

Leaving Footprints in Joy
Friday:
Luke 1:67-75

"His father Zechariah was filled with the Holy Spirit and prophesied: 'Praise be to the Lord, the God of Israel, because he has come to his people and redeemed them. He has raised up a horn of salvation for us in the house of his servant David (as he said through his holy prophets of long ago), salvation from our enemies and from the hand of all who hate us— to show mercy to our ancestors and to remember his holy covenant, the oath he swore to our father Abraham: to rescue us from the hand of our enemies, and to enable us to serve him without fear in holiness and righteousness before him all our days.'"

Turn Up The Volume!

Seems everywhere you turn there is a flurry of activity! Just about a week left to finish up last minute things, and then it will be Christmas day.

Hark the Herald Angels sing

The Costco cashier and I exchanged glad smiles when they raised the volume on the sound system. For a moment, you could clearly hear the carols spilling out over the store. It almost covered the sound of beeping registers and the noisy rush of crowds. A moment later, it was turned down again, and we were left straining to hear.

Glory to the newborn king

Sometimes the clamour of the urgent... drowns out the message that struggles to be heard.

Peace on earth and mercy mild

Everywhere we turn, the countdown is on. So much to do, say, give and receive! This season is a mixed one. Joy and festive smiles abound, but life with its struggles is no respecter of persons, seasons, or holidays. For all of those who celebrate in houses warm, with health and light, there are many, many more who sit in sadness. Loss, grief, sickness, and fear creep around their doorways. This is a difficult season for hearts all over the world.

God and sinners, reconciled

So, what do we do?   We turn up the volume!

Joyful all ye nations rise, Join the triumph of the skies

Listen to the message. Hold on to it. Walk with it, in our homes, and neighborhoods and cities. Listen for His heart, follow where it leads...

With angelic hosts proclaim, Christ is born in Bethlehem

We are loved unconditionally, deeply and passionately by the God of the universe. And we are called to Love: that is the message. Wrapped in a baby, delivered to a manger, placed in our hearts...

Hark the herald angels sing, Glory to the newborn king!

"It is good to praise the Lord and make music to your name, O Most High, proclaiming your love in the morning and your faithfulness at night."
(Psalm 92:1-2)

Leaving Footprints in Joy

Saturday:

Luke 1: 76- 80

"'And you, my child, will be called a prophet of the Most High; for you will go on before the Lord to prepare the way for him, to give his people the knowledge of salvation through the forgiveness of their sins, because of the tender mercy of our God, by which the rising sun will come to us from heaven to shine on those living in darkness and in the shadow of death, to guide our feet into the path of peace.' And the child grew and became strong in spirit; and he lived in the wilderness until he appeared publicly to Israel."

Christmas Coffee

I stirred my coffee and made myself comfortable. The small table off to the side and on its own was the perfect spot. Christmas music wafted from the rafters, competing with the Salvation Army bell and the hearty sounds of Ho-Ho-Ho from the nearby Santa's village. It was the week before Christmas at the Mall, and I had a front row seat to the craziness!

The last of my Christmas purchases were in bags, safely tucked beneath my feet. It seemed that every available inch of floor space was flooded with shoppers, flowing from one store to another in an anxious stream. It was crowded and loud, with a touch of frantic in the air!

Everyone was moving, and I suppose that's why I noticed him. He was standing still. His silver head was bent over a notebook, writing something down as he stood in front of a store window. I watched as he moved to the next display, a window filled with candles and collectibles. He had my full attention now, he had piqued my curiosity. His outdated tweed jacket reminded me of a college professor, and I wondered if he were a writer, taking notes.

I only looked away a moment, to pick up my coffee. I turned back just in time to see a hurried shopper in an oversized parka brush too close. The collision sent the notebook and pen in opposite directions, pushing the man in the tweed into the glass storefront.

It wasn't until I'd retrieved the notebook, deposited the broken pen in the trash and offered him a seat at my table, that I noticed his warm smile and kind eyes. He thanked me for my help, glad to have a place to sit and catch his breath.

"If you don't mind my asking," I ventured, "you don't seem to be shopping. Are you writing a story of some kind?"

His look grew sheepish. "No, I'm making a list"

I waited, hoping he would explain. After a hesitant sigh, he continued.

"Every year at Christmas my wife and I would shop for each other, sort of. We'd wander the mall, looking in all the windows, searching for the perfect gifts. The ones we'd buy each other if we had all the money in the world to do it with. Once we'd made a list of the items, and their location, we'd meet and go back to the stores together to see what gifts we'd "purchased" for each other. We always ended the day with Christmas coffee in the café. This year, she's not here, but I wanted to shop for her anyway."

His words faded and he looked down at his hands.

My voice caught in my throat. After a minute of quiet I managed "What a lovely idea. I'm sorry you were never able to buy each other the things on your list."

His head jerked up, revealing watery pools in those kind eyes.

"Oh no" he said earnestly, "don't be sorry. We wanted it that way. We started these shopping trips way back in college, when neither of us could afford more than bus money. After we married, most of the money went to raising our children and keeping a home. The truth is, our time together making our lists became far more valuable than anything a store could offer. There was pure joy in our yearly tradition. When we could finally afford to buy what we wanted, well, we just didn't want to give up our crazy shopping trips! Over the years we'd realized the only gift that really mattered, the only thing we really needed was our relationship and the love that lived in it. Joy and contentment grew out of that."

Seeming embarrassed by his heartfelt profession, he stared back down at his hands.

The silence lasted a bit longer this time. He fiddled with the cuff of his woven jacket, and I tried, without success, to swallow the lump in my throat. Glancing at my watch I began to gather up my bags.

"I need to get going, but is there anything else I can do for you?"

Smiling, he replied, "If you would have them bring me a cup of Christmas coffee that would be wonderful."

I told him I was so glad to have met him, wished him Merry Christmas, and stood in line to place his order.

I didn't stay to see his reaction, but I hope it made him smile. I wanted him to know his story had changed mine. I ordered him a Christmas coffee and the biggest muffin they had. I wrote on a sheet of paper, borrowed from the girl behind the counter, and I asked her to please deliver it, and a small package along with the order:

Dear Sir,

I bought this pen today, just minutes before I met you. It was a gift to me, something I've been wanting but didn't think anyone would buy for me this Christmas. I want you to have it. I hope it reminds you of the girl you met in the café. The girl who had forgotten, until you reminded her, that it's really about relationship and love.

If it's ok with you, I want to tell your story to my husband when I get home tonight. Your words may be the best gift we receive this Christmas.

Gratefully,

The Girl in the Café.

"How much better to get wisdom than gold, to get insight rather than silver!"
                    (Proverbs 16:16)

Week Four:
Leaving Footprints
in Love

Sunday
Scripture Reading:
1 John 4:7-12
The Angel/Love Candle

The prophets of old shone a light into a dark place when they promised that Immanuel would come into the world to be a Savior. Hope was now possible for people who sat in darkness and silence.

And He came. Immanuel had his humble beginning in the ordinary town of Bethlehem. His first cradle was a manger filled with hay, and those who attended his birth were a few lowly barn animals. Peace was now possible for very ordinary people in very ordinary places.

The birth was divinely announced to the rich and the poor, the near and the far. The shepherds and the wise men both came to worship the Christ child. True joy was a real possibility for all the people of the world.

All of heaven swelled with joy and amazement, and it spilled over when the angels filled the skies over Bethlehem. Heaven touched earth, and the promise God wanted to make sure the world was ready to hear, was delivered by multitudes of angels!

The book of Hebrews tells us that at many times and in many ways God spoke long ago through the prophets. But now, he has spoken his final word in His Son. What was it that God was saying?

He was saying... I love you.

This is truth:
The birth of Jesus makes hope and peace and joy possible for all people.

This is the greatest truth:
The birth of Jesus means that God loves the world.

It's a world that doesn't love God. It's a world that didn't have room for him then or now. A broken, swirling, tired world; A world that God so loved.

As you light the Angel Candle, remember that Christmas calls us to behold a God whose great love reaches out to all of us. We are part of this world, embraced by a God who loves us so boundlessly that He gave His beloved Son.

<u>Hark! The Herald Angels Sing</u>

Hark! The herald angels sing,
"Glory to the newborn king,
Peace on earth and mercy mild,
God and sinners reconciled!"
Joyful, all ye nations rise,
Join the triumph of the skies,
With th'angelic host proclaim,
"Christ is born in Bethlehem."
Hark! The herald angels sing,
"Glory to the newborn king!"

Hail the heav'n born Prince of Peace!
Hail the Sun of Righteousness!
Light and Life to all He brings,
Risen with healing in His wings.
Mild he lays his glory by,
Born that man no more may die;
Born to raise the sons of earth,
Born to give them second birth.
Hark! The herald angel sings,
"Glory to the newborn king!"

Leaving footprints in Love

Monday:

Luke 2:1-3

"In those days Caesar Augustus issued a decree that a census should be taken of the entire Roman world. (This was the first census that took place while Quirinius was governor of Syria.) And everyone went to their own town to register."

Covered by Love

It was two days before Christmas. I was standing in our new home, in a beautiful, bright kitchen, looking out the window. I was close to tears. Six months earlier after talking and praying, our family felt that it was time to move. It had been a bit of a nail biter of a process, but it happened. I knew that this was right. This is where we were supposed to be, but I was...sad, and lost.

I felt guilty for feeling like this. I should have been turning cartwheels! We had been waiting so many years to be here! Instead of joy and excitement, a cloak of uncertainty, sadness and "what if" wrapped itself around me. What if we were wrong and this wasn't where we were supposed to be? What if the kids didn't settle in? And what if (an old lie slipped in) I wasn't good enough for this?

Our puppy had died just days after we got here, and it didn't feel like home. It felt like I was cooking in someone else's kitchen. I stared out the window, and watched as a truck pulled into the driveway, changing everything...

A few years ago, my husband picked up a book titled *Traditions of the Ancients*, by Marcia Ford. It explores 3rd century faith practices, and the value that is found in traditions we have "retired." Some of the chapters include contemplative prayer, solitude, fasting and grieving.

Chapter five looks at the art and tradition of prayer shawls. I was intrigued by the tradition, and I love the concept! The modern adaptation is crocheted, or knitted. The women (or men) who make these shawls, pray for the recipients as they work on them. Prayers for blessing, healing, comfort or whatever else might be needed. The shawl is a tangible reminder of God's loving-kindness and comforting presence. When you wrap the shawl around you, you acknowledge the love of God that constantly surrounds you.

The truck in the driveway was a parcel delivery truck. I raced to the door and the driver handed me a box with my name on it! The return address was Iowa. It took a moment to figure out that it was from Linda, a friend that I met through blogging. She was in the middle of moving as well, and we had commiserated in the midst of packing boxes. Somewhere between laughter, recipes and stories, we had become friends.

I set the box on the counter with a sigh of anticipation. Inside was a prayer shawl. It was soft, warm and beautiful. A gift from a friend, a blessing from my God. A Prayer shawl! How could she have known I had always wanted one? She told me she had prayed for me while she worked on it! God knew that I needed this. It was a tangible reminder of His loving-kindness and comforting presence.

I was overwhelmed. I slipped the shawl around my shoulders, replacing the cloak of sadness, uncertainty and "what if." There would be many more days of unpacking, adjusting and settling in, but Grace would fill our empty rooms, and Love would cover all of our days! What an amazing friend, what a Faithful God!

"Yet this I call to mind and therefore I have hope: Because of the Lord's great love we are not consumed, for his compassions never fail. They are new every morning; great is your faithfulness."
(Lamentations 3: 21-23)

Leaving Footprints in Love Tuesday: Luke 2:4-7

"So Joseph also went up from the town of Nazareth in Galilee to Judea, to Bethlehem, the town of David, because he belonged to the house and line of David. He went there to register with Mary, who was pledged to be married to him and was expecting a child. While they were there, the time came for the baby to be born, and she gave birth to her firstborn, a son. She wrapped him in cloths and placed him in a manger, because there was no guest room available for them."

In Any Language

The dust on the rutted road had settled, and everything had gone quiet. We set down our bags, and looked for a place to sit. The stone steps seemed to radiate beneath us. They were the entrance for one of two proper buildings in this village on the east coast of Mexico. Our team, part of a two week Christmas mission trip, had piled in the back of an old pick-up truck and left for the next village-without us. Sun, high in the afternoon sky, baked the dirt road. It would be a couple of hours before their return, and we had no other option but to sit and wait.

Giggles broke the silence. It was soft at first, followed by loud laughter and punctuated with Spanish words. Behind us from the side of the building, children were watching, curious to see what we were going to do.

We smiled, motioning them to join us. I didn't speak Spanish. I knew a few phrases, and one short paragraph to be able to introduce myself. That took all of one minute. It was frustrating, having only those few phrases to repeat, but the children didn't seem to care.

They grabbed our hands and led us down the road, followed closely by the biggest pig I have ever seen! They laughed and chattered away in their language like we could understand every word. I wished I could have. I wanted to be able to chatter back. To tell them stories, to hear theirs, but all I could repeat was

Jesús te ama- Jesus loves you.

We spent the afternoon with those beautiful, smiling, faces. Just as the truck was returning, one little boy ran from a tin shack with a box in his hands. Skidding to a stop at my feet, he tore off the lid and proudly displayed a pair of shoes that looked just his size. They were shiny and new, a stark contrast to his worn clothing and dirt streaked face. A stream of Spanish told the story, but I couldn't understand it. Perhaps they had been bought for school, or given to him by the mission. We waved from the back of the truck, watching the group smile and wave back, the boy still holding tightly to his shoes.

We didn't return to that village, but I've never forgotten the faces, the shoes or the sound of the voices, telling their stories in Spanish.

I've often wondered what became of the boy with the shoes. So many Christmases have passed since I stood on the road repeating those words.

One simple phrase, and yet it's the most important one. Whatever language our stories are spoken in, no matter what part of the world they echo from, at the core is this: the longing, need and deep desire to be loved and accepted. The only thing that answers the cry and fills our stories with pages of belonging is this: knowing the love of the God of the universe.

I hope the boy with the shoes remembered the words. I prayed it would stay in his heart and change his story. When Christmas comes each year in that Mexican village, I hope he clings to Emmanuel as tightly as he did his shoes, and I hope his stream of beautiful Spanish words repeats the truth that he is loved!

"My prayer is not for them alone. I pray also for those who will believe in me through their message, that all of them may be one, Father, just as you are in me and I am in you. May they also be in us so that the world may believe that you have sent me. I have given them the glory that you gave me, that they

may be one as we are one— I in them and you in me—so that they may be brought to complete unity. Then the world will know that you sent me and have loved them even as you have loved me."

(John 17: 20-23)

Leaving Footprints in Love
Wednesday:
Luke 2:8-10

"And there were shepherds living out in the fields nearby, keeping watch over their flocks at night. An angel of the Lord appeared to them, and the glory of the Lord shone around them, and they were terrified. But the angel said to them, 'Do not be afraid. I bring you good news that will cause great joy for all the people.'"

Christmas Reflection

Slow down and breathe. God is still in heaven. You are not responsible for doing everything all by yourself, right now.

~**Write it down!** Having it written down keeps things in perspective. It helps organize and prioritize all the things that find their way onto the "to do" list over the holidays!

~**Take time to listen and reflect**. A fire burning to embers, wind in the bare tree tops, the sound of carols and frost patterns on window panes. God is always there, waiting for a chance to be heard.

~**Stop and observe the little things**. Seasons change, answering the call of their creator, in a steady pattern of movement, and beauty, not speed. It's not the speed at which we run this race it's in the ability to finish well.

~ **Take a day off alone**. Make a retreat, a time of solitude and reflection. Carve out time for intentional gratitude; contemplating the greatest gift to ever be given... you are loved!

~Take time to stand in awe and wonder. Without wonder, life becomes only an existence. Choose a time to turn down the lights, the volume, and the invitations. Stillness and simplicity may be the best décor this Christmas!

~Take a winter walk. Consider walking without a destination. If you walk just to get somewhere, you sacrifice the walking. Take children with you! They see things adults miss, and their exuberance is soul-nourishing!

~Count your blessings - Slowly. God's goodness is ongoing, unconditional and forever.

"How precious to me are your thoughts, God! How vast is the sum of them! Were I to count them, they would outnumber the grains of sand..."
(Psalm 139:17-18)

Leaving Footprints in Love

Thursday:

Luke 2:11-14

"'Today in the town of David a Savior has been born to you; he is the Messiah, the Lord. This will be a sign to you: You will find a baby wrapped in cloths and lying in a manger.'" Suddenly a great company of the heavenly host appeared with the angel, praising God and saying, 'Glory to God in the highest heaven, and on earth peace to those on whom his favor rests.'"

Traditions of Love

Each year around the holidays, the conversation in our house turns to menu planning and recipes. Always, at some point, someone will say...

"We are having Wife Saver for breakfast on Christmas morning, right?"

And then there is the pause, the moment where they all wait for me to answer with a resounding yes! It's always the same answer, but still they wait expectantly and look relieved that I haven't changed their favorite Christmas dish!

I have to admit, I've thought about it. Every year glossy holiday magazine covers boast menu options of all kinds. I've been tempted to change things up for a year or two, but then I remember the pause, and the eager expectant faces. I know how much they love the crazy breakfast tradition we've had since they were small. Many things have changed over the years. Grief, illness, death and location have changed the landscape of our Christmas table, but our breakfast menu remains the same.

It may not be what other families choose for Christmas breakfast, but it's a grand tradition for us, and that's what matters. It's a tradition of love, a reminder to savor the times when we are all together, enjoying each other and our yearly breakfast feast.

What traditions happen in your home at Christmas? No matter how big or small, whatever you choose to do together, may you be blessed with knowing that the greatest tradition of love we have, is the celebration of a baby's birth. As years and landscapes pass, this one thing will remain: we are loved. Overwhelmingly, passionately and completely by the God of the universe, who sent His son, to be with us, always.

"As the Father has loved me, so have I loved you. Now remain in my love."
(John 15:9)

Christmas Morning Wife Saver

Ingredients:

16 slices of white bread, crusts removed
16 slices of Canadian back bacon or ham
16 slices of sharp cheddar cheese
6 eggs
1/2 tsp. pepper 2 mL
1/2-1 tsp. dry mustard 2-5 mL
1/4 cup minced onion 60 mL
1/4 cup finely chopped green pepper 60mL
1-2 tsp. Worcestershire sauce 5-10 mL
3 cups milk 750 mL
dash of Tabasco
1/2 cup of butter 125 mL
Special K or crushed Corn Flakes

Instructions:

Set 8 pieces of bread into a 9" x 13" (23 x 33 cm) buttered, glass baking dish. Cover bread with slices of back bacon. Lay slices of cheddar cheese on top of bacon and then cover with remaining slices of bread to make it like a sandwich.

In a bowl, beat eggs and pepper. To the egg mixture add dry mustard, onion, green pepper, Worcestershire sauce, milk and Tabasco. Pour over the sandwiches, cover and let stand in fridge overnight.

In morning, melt butter, pour over top. Cover with Special K or crushed Corn Flakes. Bake, uncovered, 1 hour at 350 deg.F (180 deg.C). Let sit 10 minutes before serving. Serve this with fresh fruit and hot cinnamon rolls. Serves 8.

Leaving Footprints in Love
Friday:
Luke 2:15-18

"When the angels had left them and gone into heaven, the shepherds said to one another, 'Let's go to Bethlehem and see this thing that has happened, which the Lord has told us about.' So they hurried off and found Mary and Joseph, and the baby, who was lying in the manger. When they had seen him, they spread the word concerning what had been told them about this child, and all who heard it were amazed at what the shepherds said to them."

So this is Christmas

On December 1st, it seems there is plenty of time. We strategize each year with new ideas for peace and joy alongside our baking, gifting and growing list of commitments. We start shopping in July. We fill the calendar with reminders and memos. We start saying no to the "should do's". And all of this helps, a lot!

Still, it is amazing to me, the dizzying pace at which the season rushes by. The Christmas song, "So this is Christmas, and what have we done...." drifts through the living room, and makes me pause. What is Christmas for us? What has it looked like, and what have we done?

Sometime in November, we pack boxes for children overseas. The enthusiasm of our children as they help to bring joy to children they have never met: that's Christmas.

At least one evening during the holiday we will decide that busy or not, we are having friends in. We'll laugh, eat, and thoroughly enjoy their company. The warmth and friendship we share: that's Christmas.

Somewhere in the middle of the season, I usually realize that my sedate well-planned holiday may not be exactly as I thought. Tired and overwhelmed I may throw a fit, complete with angry words. It may be selfish, and self-centered: it's nothing like Christmas.

On Christmas Eve our family will light the final advent candle. With only that light and the light from our tree, we sing Silent Night. I usually shed a few tears, and then laugh at our children's antics and exuberance as they hang up stockings, and say goodnight. Their beautiful faces, in candlelight, filled with anticipation: that's Christmas.

Some years at Christmas my husband and I have not exchanged gifts. Watching the children enjoying their packages, my husband has leaned over and whispered "I love you." It wasn't the gifts that made it Christmas.

So this is Christmas... And what will we do? In the middle of all that is and isn't Christmas, this one thing defines it: For God so loved the world that He gave his one and only Son... not because He had to, but because He wanted to. You and I are held close in the heart of God. Love, all-encompassing, extravagant, unconditional love, was wrapped in rags and placed in a manger. There is not, nor will there ever be a greater gift, a greater truth than this: We are loved by the God of the universe: And that, my friends, is Christmas.

Leaving Footprints in Love

Saturday:

Luke 2:19-21

"But Mary treasured up all these things and pondered them in her heart. The shepherds returned, glorifying and praising God for all the things they had heard and seen, which were just as they had been told. On the eighth day, when it was time to circumcise the child, he was named Jesus, the name the angel had given him before he was conceived."

Do you hear it?

Can we stop everything to listen for the sound?
Across the sands of time and oceans of the ages it echoes on the wind. It compels us, it challenges us.

Listen.

It is comforting and forgiving. It brings hope and light. Hungry hearts are filled. Purpose and promise ring out with the sound.

Can you hear it?

It is coming from Bethlehem, from the house of bread. The greatest gift to ever grace this sphere was presented with this sound.

Listen.

Let it soak in deep, filling your heart and nourishing your spirit.

Do you hear it?

It's coming from the depths of a Love so amazing, unending and complete...

It is the cry of a baby,
The voice of the King!

"However, as it is written: 'What no eye has seen, what no ear has heard, and what no human mind has conceived"-the things God has prepared for those who love him.'"
(1 Corinthians 2:9)

Christmas Eve/Day Scripture Reading: Matthew 1.22 The Christ Candle

Our journey ends today, but it's also just beginning! What have your footprints looked like as we journeyed through hope, peace, joy and love? How has your heart been changed by this beautiful story of Love? As we lift our lanterns for the final steps on the path, let's allow this amazing truth to remain illuminated in our hearts...

Emmanuel, God **with** us.

It is not only for the season, a time or an experience. He is with us always, in all of our moments and days, speaking, hearing and loving us.

Today, may you be blessed with opportunities to welcome the promise, and listen for Love. I wish for you this Christmas, and always...

Days filled with expectant Hope. Knowing Peace, touching Grace, and flooded with Joy. Most of all, may you know, experience and be overwhelmed by the unending, extravagant, passionate Love of the God of the universe.

We are Loved!

Silent Night

Silent night, holy night,
All is calm, all is bright
Round yon Virgin Mother and Child,
Holy Infant so tender and mild
Sleep in heavenly peace,
Sleep in heavenly peace.

Silent night, holy night,
Shepherds quake at the sight
Glories stream from heaven afar,
Heavenly hosts sing Alleluia!
Christ, the Saviour is born,
Christ, the Saviour is born

Silent night, holy night,
Son of God, love's pure light
Radiant beams from Thy holy face,
With the dawn of redeeming grace
Jesus, Lord, at Thy birth,
Jesus, Lord, at Thy birth
(Joseph Mohr/ Franz Xavier Gruber)

Appendix One:

A FAMILY CELEBRATION OF ADVENT

A. The Prophecy Candle

Child 1: Long, long ago in the times of the
Old Testament, God spoke to His
people, Israel.

Child 2: God spoke in many, different
times and places.

Child 1: And God spoke in many different
ways.

Child 2:   But God always spoke through His
prophets.

Adult 1: The prophets were people who did
two things: They listened and
they spoke.

Adult 2: First, the prophets listened to God.
God told them the things that
were really important; the things
that His people needed to hear.

Adult 1: Next, the prophets spoke to the people. They told the people the things that were important to God.

Child 1: Sometimes the people of God were doing bad things.

Child 2: Then the prophets told them that God was angry and that He was going to punish them if they did not stop sinning.

Child 1: Sometimes, the people of God were sad and afraid.

Child 2: Then the prophets told the people that God still loved them and that He had not forgotten about them. He was still their God.

Adult 1: But the best thing was when the prophets told the people God's special secret.

Adult 2: God's special secret was also a promise. The promise was a secret because only those who listened to the prophets and believed what they said knew what God was going to do.

Child 1: And what was this wonderful promise?

Child 2: The promise was that there was going to be a Savior!

Child 1: No! It was better than that! The promise was that GOD was going to be the Savior!

Adult 2: No! It was even better than that! The promise was that God was going to be the Savior AND He would come down from heaven and be with us!

Adult 1: One of the prophets named Isaiah said that the Savior would be born and the child would be called Immanuel. Immanuel means "God with us!"

Adult 2: Many of the prophets spoke about this wonderful, promised Savior. And then one day...

Child 2: God stopped speaking.

Child 1: After the prophet Malachi, there was only silence..........and waiting.

Child 2: Silence.......and waiting.

Child 1: More silence.......more waiting.

Child 2: For four hundred years, God did not speak to His people. There were no more prophets. There was only silence.

Adult 2: As one year of silence turned into ten, and ten years of silence turned into a hundred, I imagine that many of God's people thought that the wonderful promise would never come true. As we sing this song, you will notice that it sounds sort of sad. Think about how hard it must have been to wait and hope through all those silent years.

Adult 1: As we light the Hope Candle you will see a burning flame. Remember that even during those silent years, some of God's people had a flame burning in their hearts that could not be put out. That flame was their faith that believed the old, old prophecies about the coming of Immanuel. And that flame was the hope that their waiting would come to an end and that one day God would break the silence.

O come, O come Immanuel!
And ransom captive Israel.
Who mourns in lonely exile here,
Until the son of God appears.
Rejoice! Rejoice!
Immanuel shall come to thee
O Israel

Let's Pray.......

B. The Bethlehem Candle

(Relight the Prophecy Candle)

Child 1: A long, long time ago, the prophets promised that there would be a Savior whose name would be Immanuel, "God with us."

Child 2: Last week we thought about how hard it must have been to wait for God to keep His promise.

Child 1: We also thought about how hard it must have been when God was not speaking to them.

Child 2: For four hundred long years God's people waited in silence. All they had was God's promise.

Child 1: Did God EVER keep His promise?

Adult 1: O yes! He certainly did keep His promise. God always keeps his promises. And that is what this week's candle is all about. It is the Bethlehem Candle.

Adult 2: The Bethlehem Candle helps us to learn some very important things about God and about ourselves.

Child 2: Bethlehem is the little town where Jesus was born.

Child 1: Bethlehem was not a very big place.

Child 2: Bethlehem was not a very important place.

Child 1: As a matter of fact, Bethlehem was a very ordinary town filled with ordinary people.

Adult 1: You know, if God had left it up to us to decide where Jesus would be born, I don't think we would have picked Bethlehem.

Adult 2: After all, Jesus was Immanuel. He was the promised Savior of the world, God's chosen one.

> Shouldn't He be born in the biggest city in the world surrounded by the world's richest and most important people?

Child 2: That is the place I would have picked.

Child 1: That is the place I would have picked, too.

Child 2: But that is NOT the place God picked. He chose little, ordinary Bethlehem.

Child 1: I guess God doesn't always think the way we do.

Child 2: Wasn't Jesus born in a stable?

Adult 1: Yes He was. Actually, it was probably a big hole in the side of a hill. People used these little "caves" for their animals: like cows, sheep, and donkeys. The caves protected the animals from the cold and the rain, and they kept their food dry

Child 1: So Jesus was really born in a barn.

Child 2: That seems like a strange place for the King of Kings and the Lord of Lords to be born!

Adult 2: You know, if God had left it up to us to decide where Jesus would be born, I don't think we would have picked a barn.

Adult 1: After all, Jesus was the most important person who ever lived on the earth. Shouldn't He be born in a special place like a castle or a palace? Shouldn't He be born in a place with shiny floors and nice furniture and beautiful paintings on the walls?

Child 1: That's the place I would have picked.

Child 2: That's the place I would have picked, too.

Child 1: But that's NOT the place God picked. He picked a barn.

Child 2: I guess God REALLY doesn't think the way we do!

Adult 2: As we light the Bethlehem Candle, Let's remember that God did keep the promise that He had made through the prophets. And even though the people sat in darkness and silence for a long time, they did see a great light because Jesus was born in Bethlehem. God ALWAYS keeps His promises.

Adult 1: And as we sing this song, let's think about the fact that God doesn't always keep His promises the way that we expect Him to. Our God thinks very differently than we do. He is full of many wonderful surprises. Many people were waiting for the Savior, but no one could have guessed that Immanuel would have been born in a barn in a little, ordinary town like Bethlehem.

O little town of Bethlehem,
How still we see thee lie,
Above thy deep and dreamless sleep,
The silent stars go by.
Yet in thy dark street shineth
The everlasting light.
The hopes and fears of all the years
Are met in thee tonight.

How silently, how silently,
The wondrous gift is given.
So God imparts to human hearts
The wonders of His heaven.
No ear may hear his calling,
Yet in this world of sin,
Where meek souls will
Receive Him still,
The dear Christ enters in.

Let us Pray...

C. The Shepherds' Candle

(Relight the Prophecy and Bethlehem candles)

Child 1: Long, long ago, God promised that a Savior would be born. The Savior would be Immanuel which means, "God with us." God made this promise through the Old Testament prophets.

Child 2: After many years of silence and waiting, God kept His promise. God the Eternal Son came to earth and was born as a tiny baby.

Child 1: Immanuel was born in a barn.

Child 2: He was born in the small,
unimportant town of Bethlehem.

Adult 1: The birth of Jesus was the most
incredible and awesome event
that had ever occurred. The
invisible God had become a
human being!

Child 1: But there was hardly anyone there
to witness this wonderful thing.

Child 2: Only Mary, Joseph, and maybe a
few animals.

Child 1: Was God going to keep this a
secret?

Adult 1: No, God definitely would not keep
the birth of Jesus a secret. That
is what this week's candle is all
about. It is the Shepherd's
Candle.

Adult 2: God announced the good news of
Jesus' birth to two very different
kinds of people. The first was a
group of shepherds who were
sleeping outside with the flocks.

Child 1: The shepherds were Jewish people
who probably knew a lot of the

Old Testament stories. Maybe
they were even waiting for the
promised Immanuel.

Child 2: The shepherds were not very far
away from where Jesus was born.

Child 1: After the angels visited them, it
probably took the shepherds a
few hours to find the baby
wrapped in rags, lying in a
manger.

Child 2: But the shepherds were also
probably very poor. The sheep
that they were taking care of may
not have even been their own.

Child1: Many people did not like being
around shepherds because of the
way that they smelled.

Child 2: I guess shepherd were not very
popular.

Adult 1: This is who the angels visited and to
whom they proclaimed the good
news of Jesus's birth: poor,
unpopular Jewish people who
probably knew the Old Testament
prophecies.

Child 1: When the shepherds found the baby Jesus, what did they do?

Child 2: They worshiped Him!

Child 1: So did Jesus only come for poor Jewish people?

Child 2: No. There was another group of people to whom God announced the good news of Jesus's birth. They were almost the exact opposite of the shepherds. They were the Wise Men.

Adult 1: The wise men were not Jewish. They probably knew nothing about the Old Testament; nothing about the prophets; nothing about Immanuel.

Child 1: The wise men lived far, far away in the east.

Child 2: After they saw His star, it probably took the wise men months, maybe even years, to find the baby Jesus.

Child 1: The wise men were also very rich. They brought gifts of gold and expensive perfume to the new born king.

Child 2: The wise men were respected people. They may have even been kings.

Adult 1: As you can see, the wise men were almost totally different from the shepherds. But there was one thing that was exactly the same.

Child 1: What did the wise men do when the found the baby Jesus?

Child 2: Just like the shepherds, they worshiped Him!

Adult 1: As we light the Shepherd's Candle, let's remember that Jesus came to earth to be the Light of the whole world. No matter what country you may live in or what language you may speak, Jesus was born to be your Savior.

Adult 2: And as we sing this song, let's remember that when we stand before Jesus we are all the same. We may be Jewish or non-Jewish, far or near, rich or poor, kings or slaves, shepherds or wise men.

When we come to Jesus, all those things fade away and we all become the same thing: worshipers who have come to adore Him.

O come all ye faithful,
Joyful and triumphant.
O come ye, O come ye
To Bethlehem.
Come and behold Him,
Born the king of angels.
O come let us adore Him.
O come let us adore Him.
O come let us adore Him,
Christ the Lord.

Yea Lord we greet Thee,
Born this happy morning.
Jesus to Thee be all glory giv'n.
Word of the Father
Now in flesh appearing.
O come let us adore Him.
O come let us adore Him.
O come let us adore Him,
Christ the Lord.

Let us pray...

D. The Angels' Candle

(Relight the Prophecy, Bethlehem and Shepherd's candles)

Adult 1: The prophets of old shone a light into a dark place when they promised Immanuel would come into the world to be a Savior. This made hope possible for people who sat in darkness and silence.

Adult 2: And it came to pass that Immanuel had his humble beginning in the ordinary town of Bethlehem. His first cradle was a manger filled with hay, and those who attended his birth were a few lowly barn animals. This made peace possible for people who live very ordinary lives in very ordinary places.

Child 1: God announced the birth of His son to the rich and the poor, the near and the far. The shepherds and the wise men both came to worship the Christ child. This made real joy a real possibility for all the people of the world.

Child 2: How did God announce this great news to the world?

Child 1: Did he send the world a letter?

Child 2: No. He announced the most amazing news of all time in the most amazing way possible. He sent angels!

Adult 1: An angel visited Zachariah and Elizabeth.

Adult 2: And an angel visited Mary and Joseph.

Child 1: And angels visited the shepherds and the wise men.

Child 2: Wow! That's a lot of angels!

Child 1: Why did God use so many angels to announce the birth of Jesus?

Child 2:   Because the message was too important to be missed. God wanted to make sure that the world was ready to hear what He was about to say.

Adult 1:   The book of Hebrews tells us that at many times and in many ways God spoke long ago through the prophets. But now, he has spoken his final word in His Son. And what was it that God was saying?

Adult 2:   If it is true that the birth of Jesus makes hope and peace and joy possible for all people then the greatest truth has not yet been said. Surely the birth of Jesus means that God loves the world. And what kind of world is this?

Child 1:   Usually, it is a world that does not love God. The world does not have room for the baby Jesus.

Child 2:   They would not let him into their homes or inns. They put him in a cold barn.

Child 1: Even though the baby Jesus was saved from Herod's evil plan, this world finally brought Jesus to the cross.

Adult 1: Indeed, this is the world that God so loved. As we light the Angel Candle let's remember that Christmas calls us to behold a God whose great love reaches out to those who do not deserve his love.

Adult 2: And as we sing this song, let us remember that we are part of this world that is embraced by a God who loves us so boundlessly that He gave His beloved Son.

Hark! The herald angels sing,
"Glory to the newborn king,
Peace on earth and mercy mild,
God and sinners reconciled!"
Joyful, all ye nations rise,
Join the triumph of the skies,
With th'angelic host proclaim,
"Christ is born in Bethlehem."
Hark! The herald angels sing,
"Glory to the newborn king!"

Hail the heav'n born Prince of Peace!
Hail the Sun of Righteousness!
Light and Life to all He brings,
Risen with healing in His wings.
Mild he lays his glory by,
Born that man no more may die;
Born to raise the sons of earth,
Born to give them second birth.
Hark! The herald angel sings,
"Glory to the newborn king!"

Let us pray...

Appendix Two:

THE FIRST DAYS OF ADVENT (2012 - 2040)

Year	**First Sunday in Advent**
2012	December 2
2013	December 1
2014	November 30
2015	November 29
2016	November 27
2017	December 3
2018	December 2
2019	December 1
2020	November 29
2021	November 28
2022	November 27
2023	December 3
2024	December 1
2025	November 30
2026	November 29
2027	November 28
2028	December 3
2029	December 2
2030	December 1
2031	November 30
2032	November 28
2033	November 27
2034	December 3
2035	December 2
2036	November 30
2037	November 29
2038	November 28
2039	November 27
2040	December 2

A Devotional Journey through Advent

~ About the Author ~

   Katharine makes her home in Ontario,
Canada where she shares life and laughter
with her husband and four children. She is
on a journey with the God of the universe,
discovering who she was created to be, and
what it means to walk living loved, in
everyday grace. She is also the author of
**Grace and Fresh Ink: 52 Devotional
Stories for the Seasons of Faith**.
   Most days you can find her blogging
through life, love, laughter, creativity, family
and faith, at ***Just A Thought***, always
listening for His heart and never without a
cup of good coffee in a great mug!

You can find out more about Katharine at:

http://www.katharinesthoughts.net

Follow her on Twitter:@kathsthoughts
and

Facebook:
http://www.facebook.com/katharinesthoughts

or visit
http://www.graceandfreshink.com

A Devotional Journey through Advent

Made in the USA
Charleston, SC
23 July 2013